Olubunmi, fondly called Bunmi, writes under the name Boomie Bol.

Born and raised in Lagos, Nigeria, she started writing at an early age, often behind her bible talking to God about world peace and forgiving the Devil. Her first memory of writing a shared poem was at age thirteen; titled "Universal Woman", it was a gift to her school principal. After years of paper silence, due to some trauma, tragedies, and misdirection. Boomie started writing again around 2010 and has since vowed never to stop. She performs her poetry and has been featured in several events including F.AT.E. 's Diaspora Monologues, and Ajilla Foundation.

Boomie shares her poems and short stories on her social media accounts and website - www.boomiebol.com - and her poetry can also be found in other publications such as Black Fox Literary Magazine. She holds a BSc. and MBA from the Northern Illinois University, and is married to her one husband. Together they have their twin daughters and continue to live and make memories in Illinois.

paper heart

Boomie Bol

ISBN: 978-1-7350408-2-0

First published 2020 Lake in the Hills, IL, USA

For Mommy and Daddy

Contents

Overview

I hope my words
Bounce from here to there
Straight into your heart

I hope they leave
The shell of my nervousness
Grow colorful wings
Flutter right into your heart

I hope they crawl
One way or some other
Two paces at a time
Until they can stand tall
Walk perfectly into your heart

I hope my words
Gyrate and twirl
Some tap to the left
Then more somersault to the right
Land square on the mark
Groove smooth into your heart

I hope my words
Bounce from me here to you there
To find room in your heart

I truly do hope this book goes beyond your hands and eyes to find room and joy in your heart. I hope you pick it up over, and over again to read. I hope a poem or two become your favorites so much that you memorize them, and they show up whenever you require them to.

These poems are stories, tales, journeys, written from the truths of my heart so it is my sincere hope they connect with yours. Behind every letter and between the lines breathes love. I write even the toughest words with, and from love.

It is this love I hope fills your heart as you read. And long after you are done reading for the first or one hundredth time, I hope the love stays. Words have such staying power, it is my hope that my words have such presence and effect.

Through each page, I hope you smile, laugh, wipe a tear or two, and relish every line you read.

Here's Paper Heart. Enjoy!

I will dedicate my first book to Grace
Grace that sought me
Grace that found me
Grace that loves me,

And

To the memory of my mother
Who saw my need for adventure
My quiet servitude
And introduced me
To books,

To the memory of my father
From whom I learned and saw
Firsthand
The most tender love
And kindness.

-dedication

I

I come from a lot of love.

-heritage

Poetry warmed its way into my heart,
First by capturing my mind.

-how I fell in love

paper heart

At dawn,
I feed my lover
With poems to grace his day.

At noon,
When he is far away
I have packed lunch
A prose or two to steadily build his pace.

At night,
He eats from between my legs
Stories of love that were softly etched
For his heart while he worked his fingers to the bones.

-nutrition

When the night
Does not love me
Like I know it can,
I make an altar of warmth
Deep within my thighs and
Slowly love myself to sleep.

-altar of warmth

paper heart

There is time between us
Days between us,

There is distance between us
Space between us,

There is lust between us
Perhaps a little bit of trust between us,

There is race between us
Caste and class between us,

I know
There is fun between us.

And sometimes
I think there just might be
Love
Between us.

The rhythm of your heart,
Births poetry in mine.

Tell your daughters you love them,
Feed them depth and the dreams of the oceans
Teach them the power that is woman
Earth was birthed by her.

Tell your daughters you see them,
Feed them joy and the hopes of the skies
Teach them the power that is woman
Earth was birthed by her.

Tell your daughters you hear them,
Feed them strength and the tenacity of rain
Teach them the power that is woman
Earth was birthed by her.

Tell your daughters you value them,
Feed them passion and the brightness of the stars
Teach them the power that is woman
Life is birthed by her.

-tell your daughters

Smiles that take your breath away,
And leave your heart in awe.

-daughters

I could have named you both
Sunrise and Moonlight
And I would be right.

I could have called you both
Red Rose, and Sweetness
And I would be sound.

I could have given you both
Names of the brightest stars,
Of flowers fair,
Or of mountains peak.

I could have named you both
Sunrise and Moonlight
And I would be right.

Or simply after nature's
Brightest treasures
And I would be sound.

-named you both

In being a mother,
Limits have been tested.

In being a mother,
Boundaries have been pushed.

In being a mother,
Patience has been acquired.

In being a mother,
Humility has been learned.

In being a mother,
Selflessness has been mastered.

In being a mother,
Love has been taught.

In being a mother
Love has been given

In being a mother,
On both sides
Love has been shown.

- in being a mother

paper heart

What a time to be a woman. A black woman.
Despite it all.

So many "it all" gets thrown at us, yet we can confidently say,
what a time to be a black woman.
What a season to be alive as a woman.
A black woman.
Renewed energy radiating self-assurance all over us.
Pushing us into spaces we once could never be. Now we own
such places and lead their charge.
Leaving trails of excellence wherever we go.
Magic goes ahead of us. Rooms fall silent at the sight of us.
Knees buckle at the sounds of our truth.
And the stereotypes that used to bind us, we crush now to fine
powder, have the naysayers blot their faces in it.
We are taking our seats at any table. Building our own chairs
where they come up short. Going beyond ourselves to leave
visible trails of magic for the ones behind us.
Lifting heads high and raising voices proud where once we
never dared.
Oh!
What a time to be a woman.
A black woman.
Despite it all.

Take me back to Dublin then Madrid,
Back to the busy shopping streets of Paris,
To the kind sidewalks of Edinburgh,
The love driven boulevards in London,
The calm and soothing airs of Bruges,
The hustle and bustle on the side streets of Lagos,
Take me back to the sandy beaches in the Bahamas,
Back to adventures and travels,
To the many lusts of wander.

I have committed to memory
Your sights and sounds
Your smell and taste
Your air.

All of you is tucked safely in me
Along with memories
Of the other places I have been.

I am thankful for this journey
To have walked your lands
Taken in your breath
Seen your parts
And experienced
Your charm.

-travels

Even after decades of intimacy, you can discover something new, in and about yourself

-eyes

paper heart

I have seen an illumination
Even in darkness,
It is the glowing
Of black girls.

-black girl magic

I knead words of courage into their skins,
I whisper words of love soft in their ears

I grace their dawn with words of blessings,
Watch them spill between sweet kisses

I seal their nights with words of rest,
Gentle lips pressed against
Their foreheads.

I speak words of bravery into their beings,
Line daily affirmations bold into their heartbeats.

I am imprinting power into their minds,
Knitting love in their hearts.

I am imprinting the love of words,
In my twin daughters.

-imprinting (the love of) words in my daughters

paper heart

Oh! little black girl,
If only you knew
The magic in you.

The one in your kind eyes,
The spark in your soft heart

The one in your bright smiles,
The hope in your bloodline

Oh! little black girl.
If only you knew
This magic is you

Its crowning glow, and glory
In your God-like skin.

-little black girl

dedicated to all the black girls everywhere

Fill my breath with your kisses
So, I can exhale as yours.

-love

paper heart

I wanted love that frees
So,
I discovered the rhythm of my heart's beats,
Listened keenly to its tunes
And found love deep
Within.

Let love fill your heart's empty spaces
Let it warm your heart's cold patches
Let love in.

Let love cleanse your heart's blotched spots
Let it soothe your heart's broken pieces
Let love in.

Let love soften your heart's hard fences
Let it ease your heart's pain filled aches
Let love in.

Let love fill your heart's empty places
Let it heal your broken spaces
Let love in.

I did not plan to smile tonight. I did not plan to laugh. But then you came along, magic in your eyes bright as the stars, and looked deep into my soul. Now here I am, my heart smiling, my belly filled with bubbling giggles, laughing, and doing all the things I did not plan to do.

-first conversations (the day you came along)

One surprise email in March…

Your hello, how is it going caught me by surprise. Between the how are you, smiley faces in all the right places…late texts, long calls, and nightly sexts…it was hard to hang up first. Two weeks and countless video chats later…we had to make it official. By August, I was your blooming sunshine. Your very able lover.

paper heart

I caught smiles with you,
In the middle of my dreams.
Wide awake from the sweet pleasures,
I kept your dimples in my eyes.

My heart was pressed to his chest in deep slumber, but even in his sleep, I heard my name in the beats his heart made.

I still do not know
How she did it.

Day after day,
Night after night,
Following a hectic time at work
And the busy life of home.

I still do not know
How she did it.

How
She was always peace.

-mother

Boomie Bol

If your body is a cave,
Let me hide in it.

If it be a temple,
Let me offer worship.

If it is a haven,
Pray, let me find refuge.

If your body is a house,
Let me forever live in you.

I like how we complement each other
You and I,

Your dimpled smiles and my freckled face
Your wit and wise,
My sweet and charm.

What a pair we are
You and I,

Like this and that,
Wit and charm,
Sweet and wise,
So, and so
You and I.

My heart,
A blank white canvas
Has your love in crimson red
Delicately written all over it.

Pumping softly,
Each beat reads
Like a beautiful love letter.

-paper heart

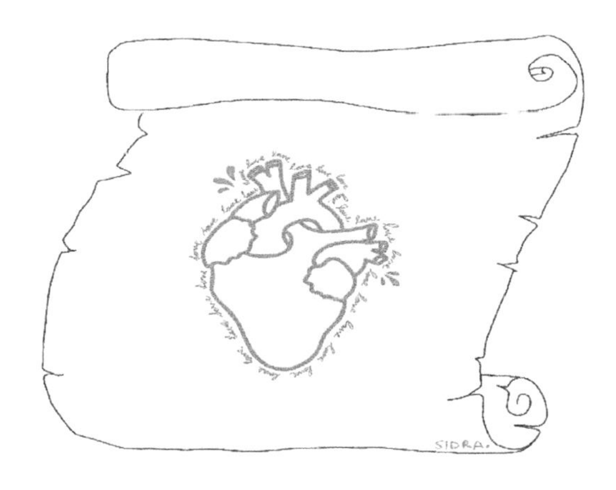

paper heart

I hide poems in me
And give him the pleasures
Of new discoveries

I would like to read you out loud
So, I can feel you for myself
In every L I N E and
Long paged
E
T
T
E
R
.

paper heart

I think you might
Have been the one
Who stole my heart away
So, I make-believe our love (life)
Picture us often
Sharing fondled kisses
And holding hands in love.

-make-believe

I am my heart's love
My soul's greatest love story
My own fairy tale.

I live on words.

So, for breakfast the most important meal of the day, I feed myself positive affirmations to start the new dawn.

Lunch is a soup of fiction with a salad of bright fantasies, and colorful adventures to take center stage. Filling my eyes with dreams, my stomach is full of wonder.

My dinner is quiet for a New York minute, meditations taking over my heart. In silence I sit for a bit…Just before audible moans escape my breath as tales of sweet erotica lull my senses to slumber.

-a day in the life of

Boomie Bol

In his eyes, and heart
In the entirety of his world,
I am the main event.

paper heart

If your love is a hurricane,
Let me be caught in it.

If it is a tornado,
I hope I find myself in its midst.

If it is a storm,
Sweep me away.

If it is lightning,
Strike hard.

If your love is a rain shower,
I release my inhibitions
And offer myself to be drenched
From head to toes.

If your love is a gentle breeze,
Blow baby, blow
Let me feel you blow.

-if your love

There is a love,
That soothes your heart to wonder

A love that flows soft then heavy
Between patterned breaths.

A love that fills your eyes
With the wonderful magic
Of knowing you are beautifully reflected
In eager eyes and tiny feet
Now cooing softly in gentle sleep.

-when they sleep (for babies everywhere)

paper heart

Mother always smelt like soap
The fresh and earthy kind,
Thick and black as night
It shone as the cover of her warm and plump flesh

Her skin soft and soothing
Like cold rains on a Friday night
Nurtured many children,

Africa, floating strength in her frail veins.

My daughter
She sits like me
Without even knowing
And I realize
I am leaving inheritances
More valuable than bank notes,
Surveyed properties, and
Weighted gold
Behind.

-inheritance

My face does not bear my parents' semblance
It does not favor them
But the soft parts of my heart,
The kindness in my bones,
The meek ways of my eyes,
These are their traits in my being
The semblance that I bear.

-inheritance ii

I am Cola and Orange
Decorated by charred tiger stripes,

The soda colors I get from my Mama
The decorated stripes from my twin daughters.

-skin(s)

They say
Beauty is in the eye
Of the beholder,
And to me
You are rainbow shades
Of beautiful.

-I am your beholder

Excuse my hair
But it is not in the mood
To be anything but
Afro

Puffed up black and proud
Roots and tips
Shining loud for all to see

paper heart

These stretch marks
Extending like the River Nile,
They are wonder tales
Stories of love like you ain’t never seen,
Or heard.

Boomie Bol

You are all my favorite
Spices and smells,
Nutmeg and vanilla,
Shaved coconut and ginger,
Hint of cayenne and a splash of lemon.

You are all my favorite
Spices and smells,
Wrapped up in stretched out dough,
Imagine cinnamon and vanilla,
With honey drizzles and lavender,
Coffee aroma wafting through the air.

-favorite spices and smells

My mother stayed back in my cheekbones
High as the love she gave
Her image and legacy
Daily reflecting
In my morning mirror rituals
A reminder of some sorts
That I am never alone.

-cheekbones

I am the dreams of my ancestors,
I am their answered prayers
Their blessed miracles

Father said;
"your journey in melanin is their redemption. You, sitting where they once never dared"
There is still far to go

I am the prayers of my ancestors,
I am their realization of hope
Their blessed testaments

Mother said;
"your journey in womanhood is their breakthrough. You, speaking and living where women before me never dared"
There is still far to go

I am the dreams of my ancestors,
I am their answered prayers
Their blessed miracles
Their realized hopes

I am the dreams of my ancestors
Their blessed testaments
Their prayers still being answered
Even now in my twin daughters,

There is still far to go.

paper heart

I hold my breath…

I listen…

To catch yours.

-motherhood

Boomie Bol

Today,
You walk into the room
And the deepest well of my soul
It lights up so brightly,
The house is charged
With vibrancy

I do not see
The unbuckled shoes,
Or displaced hairs with
Missing fine ribbons,
Nor do I notice the new yellow dress
We both picked out between giggles last night
Is now an uncertain color of mostly sand
And remnants of play.

Today,
You walk into the room
And my entirety
From the bottom of my toes
To the hairs I almost pulled out hours ago,
Rise in joy to see you
And rising joys! Do I see you.

This is the power of your presence,
The loving force of who you are,
All you mean to me.

for my twin daughters

paper heart

I have seen where the sun kisses the earth
And (there) peace is found,

Where the wind blows soft over vast lands
The noise is all air
And (here) silence is found,

Where nature is majestic brown sands,
And the bright yellow sun its crowning glory
There, and here, tranquility abounds.

I have seen where the sun kisses the earth
And leaves it glowing,
There peace is found.

-arabian desert

Boomie Bol

I am heads and tails,
Both sides of the flipped coin;
A whole selection.

paper heart

To cut the long story short,
A poem travelled down my arm
Once
Becoming ebony.

-journey thus far

A word dropped into my melanin. It travelled down into me.
It moved between my mind, and heart and found its space in both.
Then it shifted between my heart and head. It found more room in my head and dropped down into my mouth.
There it lingered soft on my tongue, but soon found its way back to my skin. Pulsating in my core
Oozing softly through my palms.

-a word

Give me love
In the laugh of a child,
In the eyes of a spouse,
In the break of a new dawn,
In the echo of refreshing rains,
In the warmth of sunny blue skies,
In the quiet rest of star filled nights,
In the hope of another good day,
In the joy of a grateful heart.

-give me love

Our reflections grab the sun's attention,
See how bright she shines when we are in her path.

Dear winter blues,
Sleet and Snow
Please be still
And cease
For my love arrives by air
On Sunday's noon,
After he's been two weeks gone
And his good loving
Is all the medicine I need
For the restless malady
Between my knees.

-chicago weather

Boomie Bol

I have tasted the sun
And warmed by its breath,
I want some more.

-golden

My mouth,
It can teach you
A few things:

1. My mother tongue,
   # Our native language

And

2. Your soft spot.

-my mouth

Boomie Bol

Love that sticks
Stains,
And leaves
Lingering
Lasting reminders.

-I was here

I have seen men spill love
From their eyes as tears,

Tears for the love they carry as pride
Within their bellies.

-true story

If then we be lovers,
Let us feast off the night
And lay till dawn breaks again

Let us kiss like tomorrow may cease
And our survival depends on it,

Let us dream like we are young
And play in the sun's delight,

Let us feed off the desire in our eyes
And the passion that binds us so,

If then we be lovers,
Let us live as such
Like the times will never end.

-if then we be lovers

paper heart

That kiss
From you
With our faces
Intertwined as one,

My breath held delicate
In your stealth hands
Felt like a moment
Prolonged in Heaven
Beholding the face
Of peace,

God himself
In our midst.

-amen! hallelujah!

I do believe
Our eyes have met
Before.

-familiar

perhaps in a life before this. or another one before that. but my eyes recognize yours.

Decades later,
And I can still taste your breath
On occasion after the first drops
Of spring's rain on my lips.

Decades later,
And I can still smell your scent
Often after a warm shower
With lavender oil on my skin.

Decades later,
And I can still see your eyes
Always after a long night
With love on my mind.

-decades later

I wonder what it would be like
If I was in your dreams again,
Tonight.

-imaginations

paper heart

He kisses me in foreign language
And my tongue is tied
Wanting only more.

-tongue-tied

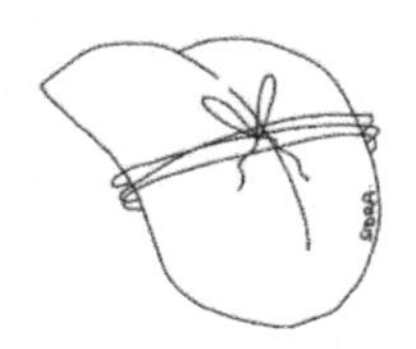

My want of you hides itself in my spine.
It bends me over (backwards)
In sweet revelation,
Whenever you are nigh.

-position

I smell good tidings
In the crisp air
Of goodwill, peace, and love
Of baked goods, food, and fun.

Then there's you,
The lingering smell of you
This is the best
Tiding of all.

-good tidings (a holiday poem)

You feel like warm showers on a cold day
Rushing down my back and thighs
I never want you to stop.

-cascade

We let go of us
But not of our love.

-feelings

Today at lunch,
between books, and empty love songs
I thought of you for a brief second,
and had to say; "*I love you.*"

-today

paper heart

The glory of the sun,
It sits pretty
In your smile.

-golden dimples

There are remnants of our love-making
On stained sheets
And supple skins.

-traces

paper heart

He sealed the night with a kiss,
And stole my heart with its reach.

-good night

How beautiful are the simple things in life?
Like your eyes in the wake of the sun's rise.

-simple things

I embrace wholly the simple things
Like hearts that smile,
And eyes that warm

Cheeks with arms spread out for a hug,
Feet ever ready for a song.

-simple things ii

Boomie Bol

In late October,
Just at the start of the fall season
The winds strip the trees bare naked,
And the leaves blush reddish brown
As they hit the cold, cold grounds.

To wake up to love radiating through warm sheets and reflected mirrors. To wake up to love breathing passion, and gratitude. To wake up to love, blissful and sublime. To wake up to love softly stemming from deep within.

-good mornings

The vision of peace. The echo of hope.
The scent of joy. The touch of love.

-senses

My palms itch,
And right fingers crawl
To pen and
Paper,
Whenever
You are near.

-muse

How he overstayed
The dinner invite,
Would forever
Be
A mystery

But here he is
Two weeks
After
That meal
Of carbs

Soft tongue
Down
My mouth.

-how?

paper heart

Don’t you know
You taught me to see the moon
Beyond its late-night glow.

You helped me see the sun
Past its midday shine.

And gave me love
Deeper than the weight
Of its four letters.

- note to a lover

Even when my heart is beating full
And the doctors claim it out of space,
I will find room for you to live in
I will create more space for you deep within.

-re-arrangements

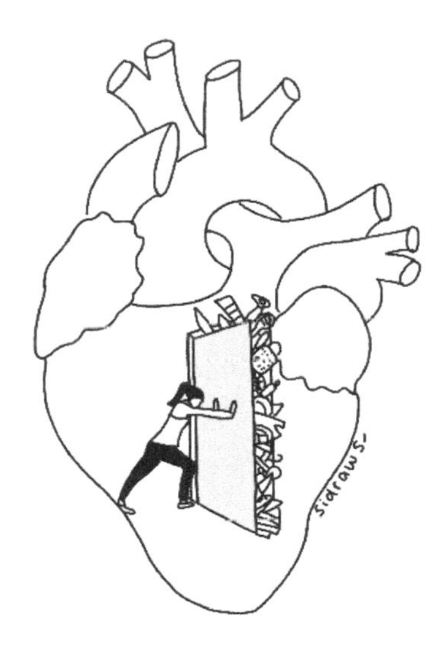

paper heart

Love beckons
In the soft and silent places
Of your still beating heart.

-listen

So many places feel like home. You, the most of all.

-you(home)

I love the look
Of you
And the way
It makes me feel,

And my heart tells me
In time
I will write
Poems
That will fill up spaces,

And share
Stories
That will keep ears itchy
To learn more
About you.

-upcoming poems

If I had a dog,
I would call her Honey
And feed her with treats.

If I had a cat,
I would call her Ginger
Or maybe Bubbles
And daily feed her fish.

If I had a man,
I would call him You,
Or perhaps Love
Often feeding you
Between my thighs
Soft and juicy kisses.

-if I had a man

I think of you and spill you onto many pages,
You are the dotted i and crossed t
In my many love stories.

-precautions

How does your skin
Warm so evenly
On mine?

How does it know
To move here, and
Here
To evoke sensations
There?

How does your skin
Warm so evenly
On mine?

How does it keep
My throat craving
More, and
More,
And even
More
Long after
Your tongue
Is done?

-how does your body know?

paper heart

It was good to hear your voice, if only through a letter. Six lines in total.

The memory of your voice echoed through each word. Each line felt like your mouth soft and moist in my right ear. Reminding me of your lips, and the magic they hold inside.

-six lines

Boomie Bol

You smell like poetry to me.
Like daffodils and lilac blooms,
Like rainbows and springtime hope,
Like morning dews and gentle rains,
Like winter's freeze and silent snow,
Like golden suns, and summer nights.

-the scent of you

When he could no longer
Hold the love in,
All the love he had long held inside,
Love that bloomed like flowers
And smelled like magic
Within his beating chest,
He let down the expectations
And cried for relief at his humanity;
Free from the notorious deceit
That real men were not supposed
To cry.

The delightful linger of first kisses.

-magic

The uncontrollable tremors as his cool fingers find your warm thighs,
And he softly goes to nibble your left ear.

-magic ii

Their first breaths were drawn
Amidst piercing wails
Shrieking from such small lungs
You would have had to cover your ears
If ever you were present in the room.

But not me,
Me
I joined them
With quiet tears streaming
Down my puffy face
And in that moment
Realized the many sounds of beauty
And again, felt the wonders of love.

-birth story

paper heart

I could not tell you
If my mother drank her tears for breakfast,
Gulped her feminine wisdoms for water,
And swallowed her pride for lunch.

I do not know if she wore silence
As her magical green-turn-red lipstick,
And blotted her aging face smooth with quiet.

I will never know if at dinner time,
She bit her tongue as she chewed on
The cow skin she could afford,
Pushing defiance back with each morsel
Mixed in with her delicious okra stew.

I will never know these things
Because life did not give us the chance,
But I know this much with proven certainty
Even now with her years gone,
In my late-night dreams
She appears as love,
Shrouded in smiles and kindness
Whispering peace to my heart.

A heart that warms,
A giving spirit,
A kind soul.

-qualities that attract

paper heart

There are words
On the edge of my lips,
My battling eyelids,
The moist tip of my tongue,
The smooth lines in my arch,
Underneath the bends of my breasts,
In the delicate lobes of both ears,
And the soft curves in my backside.

-where the words live

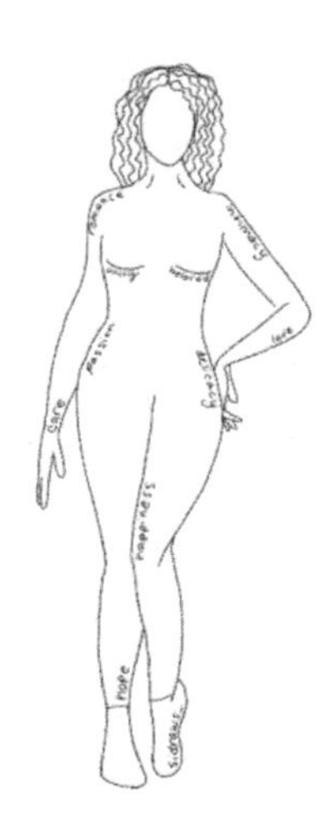

His kisses were like brandy
Perfectly aged, slightly warm

They burned and tickled
The back of my throat

And on them
I was often drunk.

-intoxication

He kissed me,
And left a tinge lingering
Long after his summer scent
Was gone.

How tender like lilies bloom
Are my thoughts of you
Each night.

-delicate

Precious black woman,
To whom can I compare you?
This allure that you give.

There is not enough time
Nor breath
To experience you.

So, pardon this consuming love,
But I offer no apologies
For wanting to love you
With every fiber of my existence
Through every second of our journey.

-renewal under the stars

paper heart

His breath moves and stills me
At the same time.

-power

Your arms are soothing,
I never want to leave them
Pull me further in.

-cover

paper heart

He grazes lightly on my left arm
And like gentle fluid love oozes out.
He pokes my bulging belly
But only more love spills out,
Not the indulgence from three nights before
Nor the meal of carbs from about an hour ago.
He hugs me tight to say goodnight
And he is stained by so much love
His crisp white shirt is now a shade of red.
He is still uncertain what I am made of
So, one last time for his own good measure
He holds my face as if leaning in for a kiss,
And his palms burn bright red
At the full contact of love.

-he wants to know what I made of (I am made of love)

We will soon be in sync as lovers
You and I
When the things that make me smile
Bring you cheer
And the things that make you sad
Bring tears to my heart.

-in sync (as lovers)

There are
Some friends
In faraway places
Whose kindness
And words
Feel so close,
So near,
You can taste their comfort
Within your breath
And almost lean in
To touch their love
Like their sweet presence
Is floating in your air.

-some friends

You tell me
To recite my favorite poem
The late night moon
Our backdrop on this lonely night.

I look into your eyes
Feel the words rush out
Like fountains of many truths
And amid these truths
You
You are my favorite line.

He remembers
My tight curves and
Soft edges,

How could he not?
Such impressions
They made,

How could he forget?
Such wonderful memories
They left,

They still
Line and trace
His late night dreams.

There's a spring to her steps,
Some swing in her hips,
A jig in her knees,
Many twinkles in her eyelids,
She means to bring joy,
This happy woman,
She means to leave joy
Wherever she goes.

-happy woman

You are fire,
Such passionate fire,
For every time our eyes meet
Or our lips touch
My soul burns.

-fire

Boomie Bol

Today's skyline
Is unusual in its display
Drawing attention to the skies
It reminds my heart of you
And the unusual ways
I still miss you.

paper heart

We will always have love. Or the memories thereof

II

In my next letter to you, I would tell you how much I love you. How much I miss you. How much I need you. But I ache, for it is far too late, and you are eternities gone.

-loss

The hurts of sudden goodbyes break hearts and sting eyes.

paper heart

My mind often wanders to our once upon a time,
Memories of happily never after painfully floating in.

These are the stories we tell ourselves
The lies we make up for our breaths
That we are okay amid the chaos
That the pain is a bearable must
And that we are doing just fine
Without their lips pressed
Against our ears.

-the lies

paper heart

It has been forever and a week
Yet you have not returned me to me.

My heart is still with you
Hidden someplace I am unable to reach
Beating in your air

    a n d
G
n   f
i   A
s   L
i   I
R   i
        n
        G
          with your breath.

I search for words to say on early morns as this,
"I love you", the only three honest words my voice can say,
I miss you another honest three tucked away in need of your embrace.

I found a new muse
But it is of no use
Either way I chose
I would still lose.

Boomie Bol

I lit a candle to blow today,
And wish you the happiest of days

The tears did not flow
For sorrow
Only for memories so evergreen
I could almost feel your breath
In my ear,

I held my own breath a while
Afraid to blow out the candle
For fear this moment
Would collapse and
Fade you back
Into nothing,

Then my tears of nostalgia
Would at last turn to sorrow
Overwhelm your happy day
And leave me to my fate.

I smell you in the air
Where you once were
And I can’t help but wonder
How the hell are you these days?

-old lover

I should have been brave
In my want of you,

I should have said more than nothing
In my want of you,

I really should have been brave
In my want of you,

Then perhaps you would have seen me
And read between the lines,

Perhaps we would have had a lifetime,
Or a week or two together.

-looking back

With him, there were no such complications. Not of
love left hanging loose in the balance, nor of love
wasted.
So, there was no reason to pick it back up.

With him, it was not a desire that was left unpursued
seeking to be reignited. No. It was never that with
him.

With him, it was just lust during periods of confusion, and
moments of weakness, years in the
making.
Lust that spelt danger and didn't deserve another
look.

With him, it was nothing more.
Just purely lust.

-looking back ii (purely lust)

1:26am!
Sleep is out of sight
And nowhere to be found
As thoughts of you flood my mind
For the fifth night in a row,

I think of us and cry.

-1:26am

Some hurts mark the lines in our faces
They become a telling part of our tales
A memory that can never be unseen
A shaping of our life's journey.

-some hurts

And what are we to do with friends
Who do not show up when we need them?

What are we to make of their silence and
Turned backs to our hurts, hearts, and loss?

How are we to reconcile our own tender hearts to
What used to be hearts we once knew, and loved?

What are we to do with friends
Who do not show up when we need them most?

Do we continue to make excuses for them in our hearts?
Do we keep the spaces they hold deep inside
Knowing we are only making up more lies?

Do we counterbalance the hurt
By counting our friends who are still here
The ones who show up and
Continue to hold strong.

When do we face the gnawing disappointment, and
Attempt to be no longer too hurt to move on?

What are we to do with friends
Who do not show up when we need them the most?

When their backs are turned on our grief?

paper heart

Does the wind carry my thoughts
Late at night to your heart

Does it say how much I miss you
And wish you were here by my side

Does the wind carry my air to your breath
To brush my smell against your chest

Does it rattle and pound
On your bedroom windows
Whispering my name
Causing your heart to contract

Does the wind carry my thoughts
Late at night and bring me
To your heart

-does the wind

I wished he never happened
Then he wouldn't get to be part of the story,
My story.

But there are no graces in regrets
So, I dub him a minor character,
An inconvenience
That could not be helped.

My once soothing pepper-soup,
It no longer warms his belly
And
His once steady lips,
They no longer find delight
Between these heavy hips.

-heartbreak

Boomie Bol

I want to feed him love
From between these, my thighs
Watch him fall fast asleep gently in my arms,
But his thoughts are stuck with another
Who's cursed him with insomnia,
And has left his appetite dead.

paper heart

How many times have I betrayed my temple
Sold myself to the highest bidder,
Seeking pleasures in the eyes of another
As my body crumbled under the weight
Of undue influence, expectations, and stress.

How many times have I betrayed my eyes
Fed it lies to soothe another's smiles,
Seeking warmth in the home of monsters
As my mind sacrificed itself
On the altar of guile.

How many times have I betrayed my heart
Given it to the wrong intentions,
Seeking life in the breath of shadows
As my soul suffered blows of disappointments
For falsehoods parceled as truths.

How many times have I betrayed my feet
Taken it on the path of others,
Seeking companionships on the wrong side
As my legs crashed and burned
On dangerous routes that led to no place.

How many times have I betrayed my temple
Fed my soul with lies and doubts,
Seeking haven in the breath of liars
Creating home in the warmth of monsters.

It was over before ever it started
But pride would not let us
Admit this defeat
So, we made a bigger mess
Of ourselves
And our time
Dancing with our pains
Around our legs
In tiring circles.

There was a time not too long ago,
When my smile was your sun's rise.

Some lovers were meant to be
Some lovers were meant to leave
Some lovers we were meant to keep
Some lovers we should have kicked
Some lovers, well those lovers
They should have never been.

-lessons

Some tears are seasonal
We shed them in their seasons
Dry our hearts, and eyes
Then pack the tears up for another day and time.

These are the seasonal tears
They come with their own reasons
And must be shed as such
Then stowed away for the next season.

-some tears

The fatigue feels as though I fell into needles
And they pushed through my pores,
Tore at my flesh and found home sticking out
In my already weary bones,
It hurts to do anything
Even drawing breath is a drag.

Sleep should bring relief through medicines
But that itself is another fight,
As my sides burn with each turn
To find the smallest level of comfort.

-fatigue

paper heart

Could the kisses on the forehead?
The gentle pecks on both cheeks
Handshakes in place of lingering warm hugs
Back pats instead of night cuddles
Could they have been the indication?
A foretelling sign
We were only supposed to be friends.

-?

What is the love that he offers
If only his mouth speaks
But his arms sleep?

He wants to pitch his tent with me,
But only a bedroom with revolving doors
He's already built a home
With firm controls,

He's met me
But a minute too late
So, there is no staying power with me,
Only this desire to pitch his tent
A bedroom with revolving doors
Then come and go whenever
As that thing between his legs pleases.

-an offer (to be a mistress)

There are old lovers that stay with us. Their scents linger in the air. Their stains on our hearts. Their bite marks are lodged as bitter tastes behind our tongues. Tastes wedged as reminders in our throats for mistakes that must never be repeated.

What assassinations happened to my soul?
How many deaths did my heart die
In shame, guilt, and disappointment
When the first hands that warmed
Between my legs
Turned suddenly cold
In strikes against my face.

-domestic violence

He was a fraud, when he whispered time and again, how much
he wanted me.
I was a fool when I believed repeatedly in contrast to my better
instincts that his want of me was good.
When I assumed all his choice words were true.

-fool and fraud alert

The crisp refreshing smells
After a downpour of soothing rains
They remind me of us, and what we used to be.

I wish you would come to me
One last time,
And give us a proper
Goodbye.

-proper goodbye

There is poetry in this too
Simple moments
Like dry leaves
Falling off
Autumn-struck trees,

Our hands fall apart
As if in slow motion
Ever so gently
As the silence washes
Over all the unsaid,

Crisp and calm
Goodbye is in the air.

Even long after our love ended,
I kept us alive on my ink-stained sheets.

-immortal (ity)

paper heart

I have seen death come and go
Too many times
As if through revolving doors.

-2018

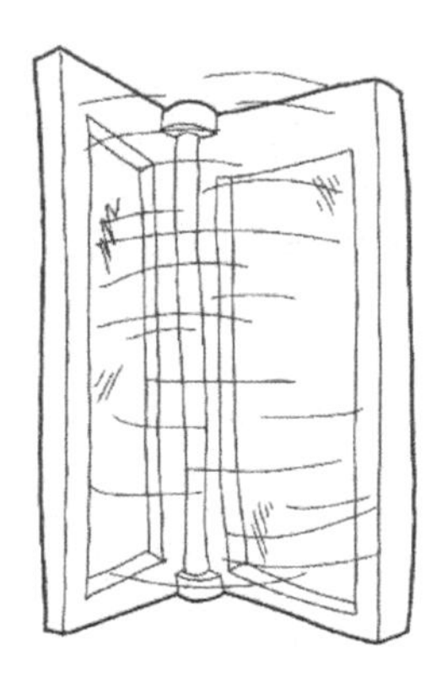

You are gone
You have been gone
But I am still here writing,
Writing about you
Poems and words
Thoughts and love letters.

On some days, I write a letter
On other days, a word…
Words
Yet in some moments
I let loose paragraphs
Long run off sentences
Proses and poems that never end.

You are gone
You have been gone
But I am still here writing.
Writing about you.

Words you will never see.

-still writing

I am in the same space as you
Breathing the air
You,
Eternities gone.

-dad

I
Am
Missing
You
In
The
Breathing
Spaces
Of
My
Heart.

The memory of you
Is a buzz in my left ear
The doctors cannot treat,
It is a pound in my heart's chambers
That medicine may never fix.

It is an unsettling in my stomach
A constant nudge in my shoulders
An itch underneath my right foot.

A deep feeling
I cannot seem to shake.

-the memory of you

I had found the first boy
Who liked me
Despite my afro
And skinny legs,

He didn't care that
I was a nerd
And had never had sex.

I was so excited,
This boy had an interest in me
My insides bubbled like jelly
At the sight of him,
Until I found
All he wanted was to be the first
Between my legs
And win the bet
Amongst his friends.

He didn't win, and I didn't lose

paper heart

First loves
Can be suspiciously tricky
When you are naïve, and teenage skinny.

So unpleasant to navigate
Your stomach unfolds on you,

When one day
You are hopelessly in love
With this person
Marking initials on oak tree barks
Your names all over wide ruled pages
Then
The next minute
Your heart is shattered tears
About how you fell
For their lies.

I wish you would stay a while and talk to me
Meet my gaze square like you once did
But your body is already at farewells
Even before my lips uttered the hello.

-firm endings (the break-up)

The memories of us they are fading away. The bedroom walls have shed your touch. The satin sheets have undone your warmth. The marble floors have un-known your steps. The pet we both named has replaced your love. The house has done away with your scent. The memories of us they are slipping away.

My heart, now unlearning your voice.

-fading

Wherein then shall we lie tonight?
On the bed of lies or the stars of night
Shall we continue with who hurt whom?
Screaming loud with each crime
Or make up for all the lost times
Find we both did wrong
Kiss fiercely and
Make up (love).

-resolutions

We will no longer pitch tents
In muddy grounds
Nor build mansions
In sinking grounds.

We will no longer give our hearts
To cold and unsteady hands
Nor give our time
To anxious and doubtful feet,
Those that seek to come and go.

We will no longer rest our eyes
In their care
Nor our warmth
In their lukewarm embrace.

-resolutions ii

I shiver and shake for your touch
I pine and pain for your warmth
I wait and wait for your love
I wait and wait and wait
I wait and wait
I fear I wait
In vain.

-gone

paper heart

It rained on the last night of us,
A symbol to ready my tomorrow's fate
The skies' downpour cleansed your scent
My heart's downpour cleansed your breath.

-goodbyes

My pain-
Thoughts of you consuming me
On nights like this, knowing
I miss you more than
I should.

My comforting agony,
You will never know.

paper heart

I have never been lucky in love,
From the fool of ’97 to
The cheat of ’03 and every
Cock, Dick, and Hairy
In between

I have never been lucky in love
So, I stayed in lust.

-no luck

She cried every time he entered and loved her.

She is taunted by the ghosts of past loves. Their bite marks are deep between her legs…they still burn after many years, and reek of the ghosts. She has scrubbed and washed. Polished and covered... She no longer peels dirty, but she doesn't see she is clean now…she was always clean, but she doesn't believe it.

She is now in the hands of good love…but she doesn't recognize it. So, every time he enters and loves her…she cries. She hasn't shaken the ghosts of past loves loose…

She is not sure how.

-remnants of abuse

There in the empty spaces between us are more words that should have been said. Softly uttered if at all; not merely felt. But we left the silence to fill in the blanks. We let our assumptions take down our truths.

-our undoing

I miss you just enough not to want to come back.

-afar

I suppose in the end, we will learn to love, and be again. In the end, it all will make sense. But until then, we will hold our breath and let these tears fall because the pain is deep. Deep within the bone marrow, and like penetrating shots, it hurts to the core.

-pain and loss

Tears shed from a broken center
Echo pain in the still of winter
His love gone cold now lies
Warm
In the arms of another.

paper heart

How can I find rest in your arms?
When I can hear the beats of your heart
Calling strong for her.

-how can I?

I carry grief
In my spine and left eye,
Because of its heavy extent
It has spread across my lower back,
And left my posture tilted to a weird angle
I could never again stand up straight.

Then there's my left eye
Slowly shutting on itself
Even behind the thick and
heavy frames.

-side effects

paper heart

I find that I am still thinking of you, and I can no longer help myself. You have left me weak where it matters the most.

You have turned my already soft heart so weak in need of you.

Abuse hides in places of innocence,
Between cousins and make-belief,
Uncles who want to taste your breath,
And dirty old men who call your father friend.

-abuse

How many are living
In the shadows of the night
Hiding in plain sight during the day
Faces hidden from the light
For fear of recognition
And retribution
After years of running
Swollen red eyes always
Looking back
Over slumped shoulders?

How many are living
In the shadows of the night
Hiding in plain sight during the day
Afraid of the dawn's light
Cursing the sun's rise?

-abuse ii

The sun is cold
In your eyes.

-hate

My love
Does not come to me anymore
Not at dawn nor at dusk.

His love has gone cold
Same as last winter's freeze
His brown eyes are void of warmth
Even under the blue flames
Of the night's fireplace.

His sweet pleasures
Are nowhere to be found.
His once warm hands
Are now cold to the touch.

His presence,
Is but a flick of the night's wind.

I once had plans to make you mine.

-old news

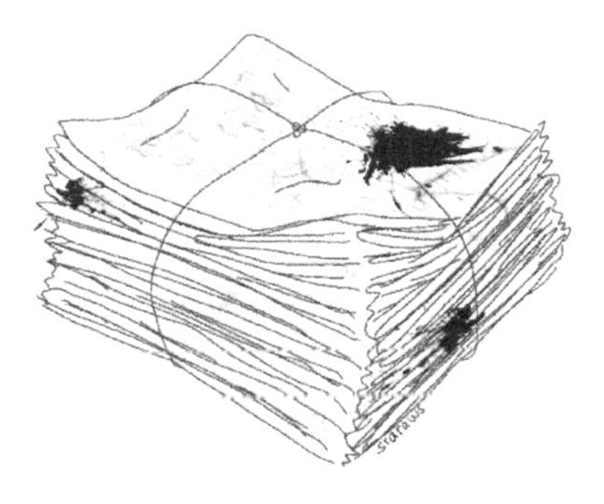

paper heart

I took a trip past memory lane,
And there you were living,
Laughing, and
Moving on
……………….

I had to ask myself
"Why, I was still holding on?"

There are now no longings
In my thoughts of you,
I have packed the last tears away
Saved for a better love(r).
The sun is glistening after the heavy downpour
And I have pulled hope from its bright rainbows,
Tucked safely in forgotten are the memories of you
A new realization is emboldened
There are now no longings
In my thoughts of you.

-moved on (over you)

I hope in time to come
When you think of all the
Undeserving love I gave
Freely and of myself
To you,
I hope you will remember
What good it did your heart
And pay it forward.

-cycle

Boomie Bol

What are we to do
When all our love burns out,
But the world does not end?

There is bravery in goodbyes,
Realizing the ending of things,
Taking your bow, and
Bidding farewell.

-the end

III

And who knows,
Perhaps the pains will break on themselves
And our hearts will heal again.

-wonders

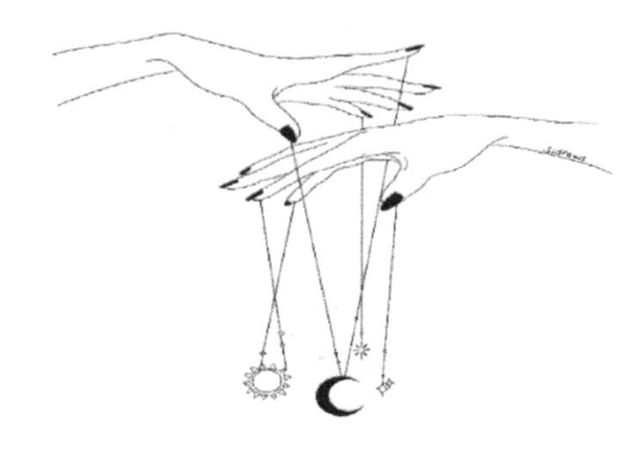

You are now absent from my breath.

-healing

The healing must begin somewhere,
Why not within me?
Why not with me?

Boomie Bol

The troubles
They tried to keep us
From dreaming
From laughing
From living
Surviving seemed darn near impossible.
But look here,
The troubles they keep trying
As we continue
Dreaming
Laughing
Living
Surviving
Thriving
Doing all the darn near impossible.

paper heart

Far be it from us,
That we only speak to the pains
When there have been too many joys
Along the way.

If ever they want to come back after making a mess of your heart. After muddling up your life. Let them know you have done well cleaning up their mess. You have scrubbed their acts and time away. You have packed their garbage into the fire. You have done away with their stains on your cheeks, and your breath. You are now breathing clean air.
The slightest speck of dust is no longer tolerated.

paper heart

I have nothing for or against them
Except
For love,

Love

From a safe distance

-to the abusers

This is the brilliance of me,
This being that I am becoming

- I know love
  Beyond a man's name.

Even after the abuse
The tints of evil you left,
On the walls and bathroom floors
On my face and in my core,

I am still flowing soft
Like gentle streams
Soothing the hands that touch me
Giving love to all around me.

-still soft

I helped myself heal
By getting over you.

-self-preservation

paper heart

On painful days
My heart whispers to me;
"Let's write"
It beckons;
"Let's write some more."

Some people leave,
And we heave
A sigh of relief.

-free

At long last
The spell is broken
The curse is reversed
I no longer miss your face
I no longer crave your touch
And on quiet nights like this
I no longer think of you.

-free ii

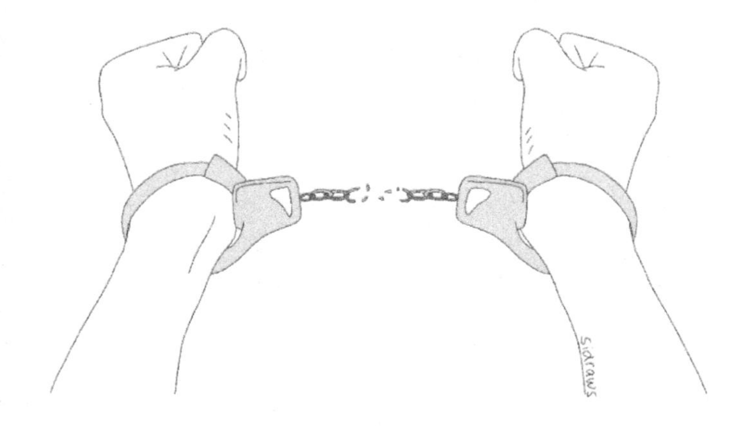

In the breath of words
Resides powers,
Speak them
To inspire.

After pain so crippling
We come up for air,
We breathe
Again.

-reminder

The night is dark and cold,
But I will not mark it as cruel
Seeing as it brings me (some) rest
Ahead of the day's light and warmth.

-perspectives

What shame is there
In the home that
Shelters your soul?

-body image

Stop picking yourself apart,
Carving out territories on your body parts
And turning them one against another.

Stop creating wars on your body,
Pitting legs against chest,
Breasts against belly
Causing your heart to beat
Beyond its might and reach
The right side pounding like giant winds
Against the once quiet left.

Stop focusing on what is gray
Or sags like a bag of stale potatoes,
What used to be there,
And what you think now sadly
Remains.

STOP!

Stop picking yourself apart,
Stop creating tragedies
In your sacred spaces,
Marking out territories on body parts,
And naming them less than truths.

Your body is a temple,
Your safe space,
Your true home,
And in this zone,
Violence and wars
Should not exist.

There will be tears,
But there will also be joys,
Smiles, and boisterous loud laughs
And by God,
May there be many more
Boisterous loud laughs that crack the ribs
And bring tears to the corners of the eyes than
There are pains
That bring tears, and sorrows to the heart.

Listen!
The trees are speaking courage
To your bones.
The grounds are thumping might
With your strides.
The birds are chirping beauty
In your heart.
The winds are blowing rest
For your soul.

-listen!

I forgive myself
For whatever role I played
In my past.

I forgive my past
For whatever the hurt it was
In the grand scheme of my life.

I forgive the perpetrators
The ones who made my past
A hurt that haunts
However big or small
And made a mess of that time of(in) my life.

I forgive myself
My past, and
The perpetrators,

Because the healing
It must start somewhere.

-I forgive

I believe infinitely in kindness. In its high power and might. In the extent of its reach, because in the simplest of ways, in the weirdest, most unassuming, and unexpected of ways, like wildfires, it catches on.

-the infinite power of kindness

Laughter, is like potent magic
Contagious and strong.

It comes in
Spreads itself about
Filling up the space it takes
And suddenly,
Like quick poison you feel it effects
As burdens shift,
Once heavy weights become lighter,
Dull moods brighter,
The encompassing air better.

-the possibilities of laughter

The generous act,
The simple smile,
The offer to listen,
That tight warm hug
The kindness you give
To that stranger
Or friend,
It could be their miracle
The long-awaited answer
To their never-ending prayers.

-you are someone's miracle

Our weapon is love
And the victory is in more than their defeat
It is greater than the surrender of the opposition,

It lies also in our unity
The coming together of all sides
For a better and greater good.

Boomie Bol

We are not the kind of magic they seek,
But we are magic alright
We just know now for whom and what we must glow,

No longer do we seek to please the snap of their fingers
No longer do we look to their eyes for permission
Our foremothers did that
To no great end,

We are their daughters alright,
But they have sharpened our mouths
Spilled strength into our eyes
And straightened our spines to tall
In dark corner rooms,
While they bit their tongues and
Took the abuse,

We are not the magic they saw,
But we are magic alright
Daughters of our foremothers
Their unused magic joining forces with ours
To define a new era.

paper heart

I poured poems
Like saltwater
To these burning wounds
Your hurt left me.

In time
They slowly healed
Themselves,

With only scars left
Scars that now bloom
On occasion like flowers,

And serve to remind me
Of the potent
In my art.

I want to make love with the lights on, so the monsters know, I no longer have anything to fear.

-roads to healing

Dear mirror, mirror on the wall
I do not need to be perfect
Nor do I need to be all together.
I do not need to be unflawed,
Spotless, and pristine.

What I need,
Is to be authentic with my imperfections,
Brave in my flaws,
Confident with my spotty areas
Content with who I am

Working with progress
Towards the most genuine version
Of me.

-dear mirror (mirror reflections)

My solitude has taught me peace
Peace within and on the outs,

It has taught me to listen
To the quiet, and the echoes.

It has taught me contentment
The joy of being with myself,
The satisfaction in my own company,
The love this can build.

-my solitude

And when they have stepped
In our shoes
Taken the fearful steps,
The faith-filled strides,
Both giant, and small
Then
And only then,
Can they begin to comprehend;
The breadth of our journey,
The length of our tumultuous walk,
The weariness along the paths,
The fatigue in our legs,
The bruises on our feet,
And the now
Slowly building spring
In our steps.

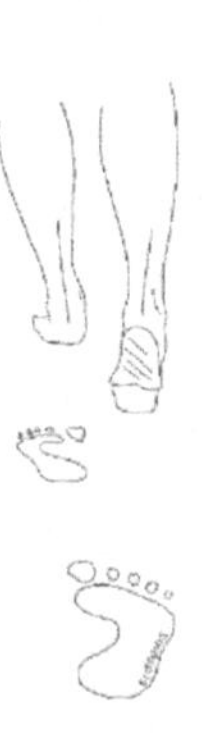

Boomie Bol

Time soothes aches
Forever woven in our hearts
Memories seek to fill the void.

There is no more anger towards you. In its place now lives peace. Forgiveness, kind and calm. Healing, slow and steady. Hope that once hung like a needled thread now hangs sturdy, as a cord of thick strands.

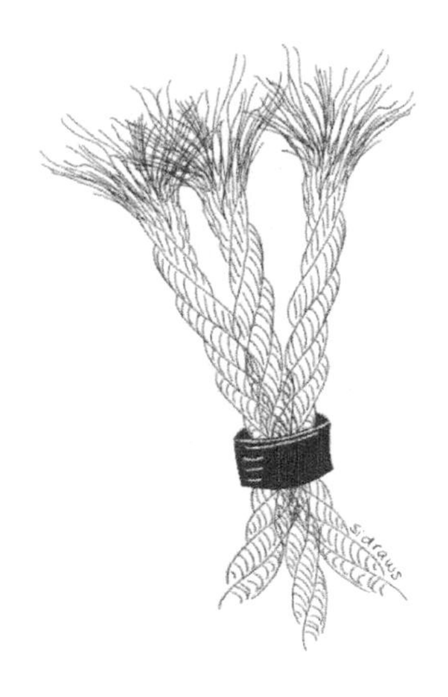

I am speaking out the ills,
Spitting out the weights,
Healing from within.

-therapy

On some days
We require words
That will soothe our souls,
Reminders
That we are never alone.

-prayers

Protect your peace,
You will need this space
For the days, and roads ahead.

Who knew there was salvation in single sentences?
In small words?

-journaling

Top on today's agenda,
Number one on my never-ending to do list,
Is to smile.

In this moment,
Somewhere out there
In this big and diverse world,
Someone is thinking good thoughts
Of you.

Heal
Forgive
Let go
Move on.

-to do list (it takes time but make time for these)

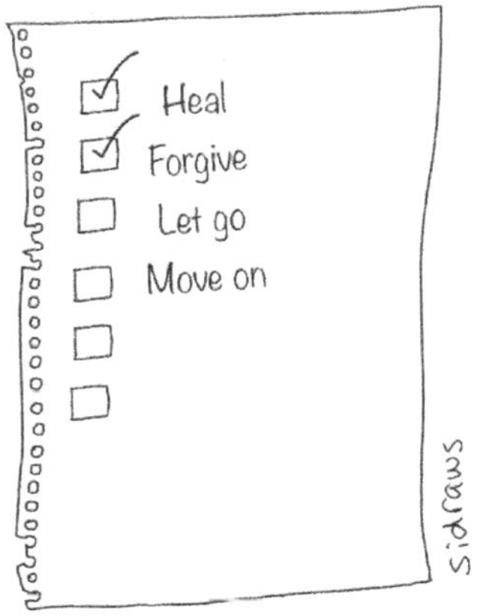

Kindness lives in bones.
It is strength that moves.
It breaks in betrayal, wears brittle in hurt.
Tend gently to your bones,
They ought to carry you far.
Beware of bone crushers.

-kindness

There is no shame here
We have long embraced our flaws
We know who we are

paper heart

I am blinking into words
What should have been tears,
Let it not be said,
I didn’t give this craft
My all.

Let it never be said
I wasted any part
Of my misery.

Do not let regrets fill the void
where memories should have been.

...and just as we were about to tumble
Fall off the ledge of all our troubles
To break into several million pieces
Of shame, and nothingness,
We found ourselves instead
Free-fall tumbling,
Not into despair, and nothingness
But into renewed hope,
Into newness,
Into strength.

-we fell to hope

Boomie Bol

The days that once scarred us,
We remember now
With strength in our hearts.

paper heart

Today I craved intimacy
So, I sat down with myself
And listened intently,
With fondness,
To my heart.

Boomie Bol

How delightful
This ability to laugh,
Despite it all.

paper heart

Even in the nail-biting
Last-second buzzer moment
Hope can still prevail.

Boomie Bol

I took the broken pieces of my heart
Twisted, and turned them around
Making beautiful pieces of my art,

Look how the hurt from last winter
Splatters tears as decadent healing words.

The pains from junior high
Formed into soft inspiring poems,

And the violent decades
Of abuse could have been shame
But here they twist,
Displayed in magnificent story telling
That inspire many.

paper heart

This is how
I am warrior,

This is how
They know my fight,

When I stand unfazed
Oozing love, and kindness
Amidst all the hate and guile.

Sometimes we must go back
To be some version of whole again.

-closure

paper heart

I am healing
In all the right places

Spaces where your hurt
Left stains
That seem to linger
Long after
The goodbye.

In my head,
And in my mind

In my heart,
And in my arms

On my sides,
And down my thighs

In my mouth,
And deep down
My throat.

Out of the hiding spaces we crawled
Into the open air
To find there was much living
To be done after we freed,
And forgave ourselves

Leaving the past
In what we once thought
Were shelters,

Cages that only held
Us back.

I stood up to the fear of losing you
I emerged the victor.

-survival

We tell ourselves
In the end it will be alright,
Antsy fingers crossed for days unknown
But what do we know as fate unfolds?
Dawn revealing varied thoughts, and deeds
Faith trampled or tackled.

We tell ourselves
In the end it will be alright,
Fingers crossed with each battle won
What will be next we wonder each time?
What will be next we ponder out loud?

We tell ourselves
In the end it will be alright,
But what do we know as fate unfolds?
For all too soon night falls, and we drift off to slumber
Dreams numbing doubts
All the while reassuring minds
In the end it will be alright,

But what do we know
As fate unfolds?

Yesterday whispered faintly
Into today's dawn;
"there's still much living
for her to do, she has not given up yet"
So,
Today vowed to do her best
To bring new-found strength
Into my morning breath
In preparations for tomorrow.

-the days whisper amongst themselves

Cleanse your breath of him with sweet wine,
Scrub between your thighs with black soap,
Be rid of his smell down there,
Purify with incense if need be
The thoughts of him
That held you still.

Tend to the bones he picked apart,
Listen to your heart's ache from the pain he caused,
Hear out your mind as it seeks not to make the same errors,
Purify with incense if need be
The thoughts of him
That broke you down.

Dry the tears as they come,
But let them fall freely as they cleanse your being,
And release the breaths you long held in
Because of his undue expectations,
Purify with incense if need be
The thoughts of him
That held you ill.

Breathe the free air of your newness,
Allow the rains to fall all over your curves,
Let them clean the marks, and places he once touched,
Walk again where you never dared,
Purify with incense if need be
The scents of him
That held your breath,

Now, watch your soul be free of him.
-purification

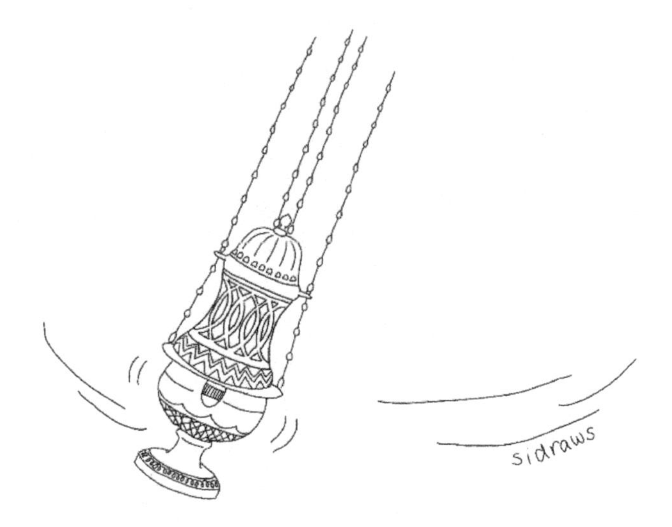
sidraws

My dead may not return to me,
But perhaps I can wish them hard
With eyes closed, tears shed, and prayers said
Into my dreams
Tonight.

Yesterday, there was an image of you in my cup of joe, and then again on my bathroom tiles. At noon, it was in my bowl of soup. But instead of flooding my heart with tears, I brought out my pen, and wrote.

-making lemonade

Even with the many heartbreaks, our hearts still remember the feel of love. They crave its touch and want some more.

Celebrate me, and these words here. While I still have my being, and while the source still flows. Celebrate me, and these words now.

For far be it from me, that the glories should come after I am gone, and the consolation lies in what could have been.

Show the new fears
What happened to the old ones,

How you overcame
You overcome,

And how you are ready to face
These new ones
Faith first.

-overcoming

Unlearn the fears. Wash out the doubts. Purify your mind.
Cleanse your soul. Heal your heart. Give rest to your eyes.

-rituals

Boomie Bol

Who knows what the afterlife looks like?
If there will be velvet red cupcakes,
Ooey gooey pizza,
Cotton candies pink, and sweet,
Spaghetti so saucy you stain your tees,
Smack your lips and beg for more.

Who knows what the afterlife looks like?
Not you, not me
Nor have the ones gone come back to tell,
So, live a little in this moment you are assured
Delight your guts,
Eat that cake already.

To know freedom within your own mind,
Love within your own heart,
Rest in your own arms,
Joy in your own eyes.

-liberation

Un-hurry your day,
Let the nights soothe you.

-rest

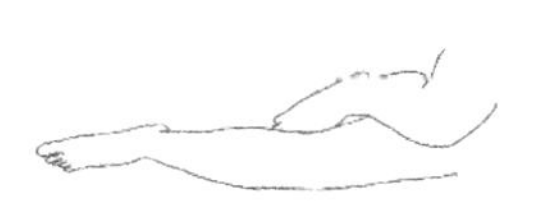
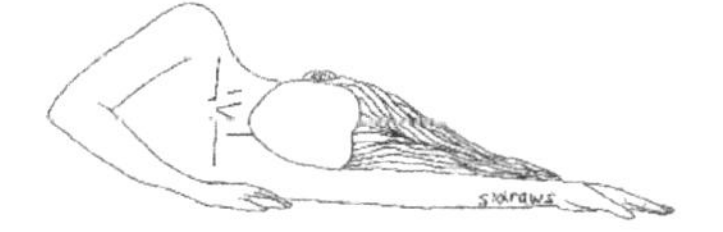

There is bloom
Soft, and gentle bloom,
Underneath all the rubbles
Of winter's breath and unrest.

There is warmth
Tender, and soothing warmth,
Beneath the heavy layers
Of winter's tights and scarves.

There is hope
Bright, and loud hope
Underneath the hollow shades
Of winter's dark and clouds.

There is bloom
Soft, and gentle
Warmth
Tender, and soothing
Hope
Bright, and loud
In the near horizon.

-spring

See!
We can still laugh again
From the bellies of our souls.

It might seem unbelievable now,
But give it time
Feed it faith
Do not give up,
Or give in
We will still laugh again
From the depths of our souls.

She is deemed wise
The woman who knows
At the sight of a new dawn
She must break into song

-gratitude

Those of us who grew up swallowing our words like morsels of chunky food, beating at our chests to keep them down: We must put into words what decades of shame have done to our core. We must spit out all those words buried underneath our intestines. We must speak now, even if through pens, since we have been groomed for so long into silence, we may not know how to speak up for ourselves.

But our mouths should only be still if we please; we know now there is no shame if the words want to pour out like rushing waters from inside us.

Here we were
Thinking the rains were
A reminder of our tears
The gathered storms
A perfect synchronization
Of sorts
For our hearts' pain,
When in truth,
The rains were a cleansing
A doing, and washing away
Of our hurts
For renewal, and
Growth.

-blessings

For me, there are now no regrets at the end of us,
for you come back, time and time again as words.

-no regrets

Acknowledgements

If my words have done you good,
Lifted your spirits on an occasion or two.
Do me this good deed, I beseech
A great kindness, if you please;
Say a prayer on my name,
Burn an incense for my sake
Pray my wells never run dry.

Thank you so much for reading! I truly hope each page was worth every penny spent.

To whom much is given, much is expected. You have given me an avenue to share, I hope your expectations were met.

All thanks to God for this dream come true in a season that seemed less than ideal. What a journey this has been. Thank you, Lord.

I am a product of the most amazing parents, and family. I cannot speak enough of this good fortune.

To my mother, who introduced me to books, and loved me with every breath in her body. I love and miss you every day. I wish you were still here. I am so grateful to have been your daughter, and only wish that we had a longer time together. Better yet, I wish I made better use of the short time we had together.

To my father, the oldest and deepest love of my life. To know you is to love you, and I love you absolutely. It breaks my heart that you aren't here anymore. It is an understatement to say I miss you, but with every breath in my body, I do every day. I am so thankful for the life, and love you gave me. My heart misses your presence and your voice.

To my siblings, Seyi, Gbenga and Dupe, Olumide and Fola, Seun (my editor-in-chief) I love you all to my core. Thank you for always being there for me, I wouldn't trade any of you for all the world's treasures. You are my many greatest treasures. I know this has been an eye-opening and most difficult season, but we have each other so it makes life easier. We are enough.

To my nephews, and nieces, your second coolest aunty loves you all. You make me so happy.

To my dear husband fondly called Mr. B, thank you for loving me through my mess, stress, and the insecurities. You are a mighty good man. I love you.

To the most important beats in my heart, the best things I could ever do; the ones who brought words back on a cold December night. My darling twin daughters, my best friends, and absolute prides, I can never say or write it enough but here I go again, PK, PJ I love you both so much it hurts and delights my bones. You are the best poems I could ever write, the greatest stories I could ever tell, my top two favorite humans. Thank you for loving me back. Your eyes are my joys and truths.

To my friends, you know who you are, thank you for the amazing journey in friendship. You have held my hands, lent your hearts, and offered your ears. I am thankful for all your love, choice words, and forever support.

Thank you so much Ken Powell for always encouraging me to keep at this and taking your very busy time to read and edit this several times. You are a beautiful definition of kindness, and greatly appreciated.

My heartfelt gratitude to Toyin Adebiyi and Sangeetha Alwar. It truly takes a village to birth a dream to life. This dream could not have been born without your efficient efforts.

Thanks Sid for the beautiful illustrations.

To everyone who continues to love and support me, I am grateful for you. Thank you.

I am forever grateful to words. In them I have found peace, solace, and joy even on my darkest days.

Love and light with absolute gratitude for always.

Thank YOU!

For more of Boomie's work, follow her online here:

Website- **www.boomiebol.com**
Facebook- **Boomie Bol**
Instagram- **@Boomie Bol**
Twitter- **@boomiebol**

Sidra Afzal is an ambitious graphic illustrator and digital artist. She loves spending her time writing poetry and creating art. She can be found on Instagram- **@sidraws_**

Made in the USA
Monee, IL
07 November 2020

46915602R00163